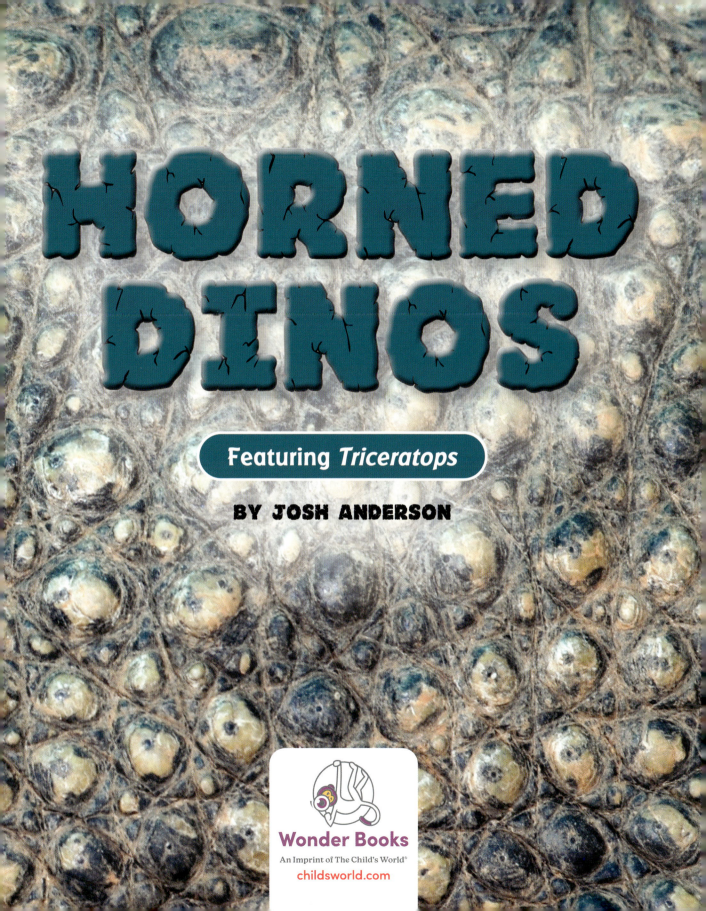

HORNED DINOS

Featuring *Triceratops*

BY JOSH ANDERSON

Wonder Books

An Imprint of The Child's World®
childsworld.com

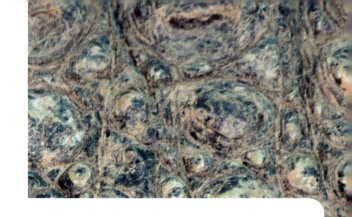

Published by The Child's World®
800-599-READ • www.childsworld.com

Photography Credits
Cover: ©avajjon/Getty Images; page 1: ©Pan Xunbin/
Shutterstock; page 5: ©Stocktrek Images/Getty Images;
page 6: ©Artush/Getty Images; page 9: ©Pier Marco Tacca/
Contributor/Getty Images; page 10: ©MARK GARLICK/
SCIENCE PHOTO LIBRARY/Getty Images; page 12:
©herraez/Getty Images; page 13: ©Stocktrek Images/
Getty Images; page 14: ©Andrea Ferrari/NHPA/Photoshot/
Newscom; page 15: ©MARK GARLICK/SCIENCE PHOTO
LIBRARY/Getty Images; page 16: ©Tuul & Bruno Morandi/
Getty Images; page 16: ©Julio Francisco ; page 17: ©Julio
Francisco; page 19: ©EvgeniyShkolenko/Getty Images; page
21: ©Xinhua News Agency/Contributor/Getty Images

ISBN Information
9781503865259 (Reinforced Library Binding)
9781503865877 (Portable Document Format)
9781503866713 (Online Multi-user eBook)
9781503867550 (Electronic Publication)

LCCN 2022940983

Printed in the United States of America

About the Author

Josh Anderson has published more
than 50 books for children and
young adults. His two sons, Leo and
Dane, are the greatest joys in his
life. Josh's hobbies include coaching
youth basketball, no-holds-barred
games of Exploding Kittens, reading,
and family movie nights. His favorite
dinosaur is a secret he'll never share!

CONTENTS

CHAPTER 1

Digging for Bones

Pretend you can time travel to a prehistoric age . . . . You have gone back about 70 million years to a grassland in North America. A horned creature about the size of an elephant is eating from a short bush. It is *Triceratops* (try–SAYR–uh–tops). Suddenly, there's a loud noise behind you! The dinosaur turns and lifts its large horns at a charging predator. But it's not just any predator. The huge dinosaur charging toward *Triceratops* is *Tyrannosaurus rex* (teh–ran–uh–SAWR–uss REKS). In a flash, it jumps on *Triceratops*. The giant beasts tangle in an epic showdown.

How do we know that two of the most well–known dinosaurs from millions of years ago fought? The simple answer: SCIENCE! Let's learn more!

Triceratops and T-Rex are two of the best known dinosaurs.

A *Triceratops* skull is around 10 feet (3 meters) long.

Humans have been studying *Triceratops* for more than 130 years. The first discovery of a *Triceratops* **fossil** was in 1887. It was found near Denver, Colorado. The bones were part of the creature's huge skull and two horns. The fossils were sent to a **paleontologist** named Othniel Charles Marsh. Marsh first thought the bones belonged to a prehistoric bison. A more complete skull fossil was found a year later. Marsh realized it was a dinosaur. He named the new **species** *Triceratops*. The name means "three-horned face."

Since 1887, many *Triceratops* fossils have been found in North America. Its fossils are some of the most common discoveries in the dinosaur world.

The largest *Triceratops* skeleton ever found was nicknamed "Big John." Big John was found in South Dakota in 2014. Its skeleton is about 60 percent complete. That means paleontologists were able to find more than half of its bones. Using the fossils, scientists have learned how Big John may have lived . . . and died.

Triceratops's skull included a large piece called a frill. The frill may have protected the dinosaur's neck. Big John's frill has a hole in it. Researchers think it was caused by the horn of another dinosaur. Maybe another *Triceratops*! They can even tell that Big John was attacked from behind. Scientists have a **theory** that Big John died several months after the attack. He likely got an infection caused by the wound.

Scientists think Big John probably weighed about 12 tons (10.9 metric tons).

Triceratops used its beak to grab and pluck leaves from trees and bushes.

CHAPTER 2

What We Know

Triceratops belonged to a group of dinosaurs called ceratopsians. All ceratopsians had a bony frill at the back of their skull. They also had a parrot-like beak for grabbing and eating plants. *Triceratops* was big, but it wasn't the largest ceratopsian.

When It Lived: 66 million years ago – The Late Cretaceous Period

Where It Lived: North America; grasslands

First Discovered: 1887, Colorado

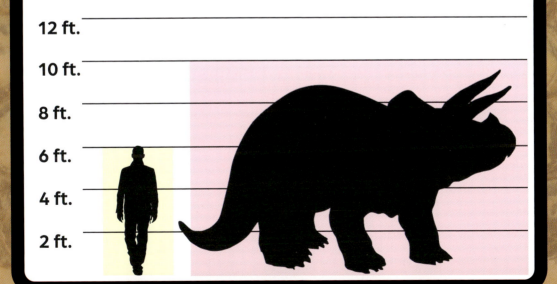

12 ft.

10 ft.

8 ft.

6 ft.

4 ft.

2 ft.

Triceratops was a herbivore. It ate plants. It had a lot of teeth and a strong beak. This meant it could eat rough, thick plants. It may have used its horns to knock over taller plants. *Triceratops* was one of the dinosaur species that lived until the **K–T extinction event**. That event likely led to the end of the dinosaurs.

FUN FACTS

- The name *Triceratops* means "three-horned face." The dinosaur had a short horn on its nose and two long ones over its eyes.
- A *Triceratops* head measured one-third the length of its entire body!
- *Triceratops* had up to 800 teeth.
- The horns above the dinosaur's eyes could grow to be 3 feet (91 centimeters) long.

THEN AND NOW

It was once thought that *Triceratops* walked with its legs out to the side, like a lizard. But a new study of *Triceratops* footprints has helped to change that idea. Many scientists now think that *Triceratops* walked with straight legs tucked underneath its body.

Scientists believe *Triceratops* moved very slowly due to its large size.

The points on a *Pentaceratops*'s frill made it look like it had five horns.

Triceratops wasn't the only horned dinosaur. Here are a couple others from the ancient world:

Centrosaurus (sen–troh–SAWR–uss) was a dinosaur whose name means "sharp–pointed lizard." It probably weighed much more than *Triceratops*. It lived a few million years earlier too.

Pentaceratops (pen–tuh–SAYR–uh–tops) didn't really have a "five-horned face." That's what its name means. But it did have three horns and one of the longest heads of any dinosaur. Its head could be almost 10 feet (3 m) long! *Pentaceratops* lived earlier than *Triceratops*.

UP FOR DEBATE

Scientists aren't sure if *Triceratops* lived alone or in groups. In most discoveries of *Triceratops* fossils, the animal was found by itself. But a 2005 dig led some scientists to think otherwise. The bones of several younger dinosaurs were found at the dig. Some scientists now believe that *Triceratops* might've lived in groups, especially when they were young.

TRICERATOPS

(try-SAYR-uh-tops)

VS

Length: 30 feet (9.1 m)

Weight: 15,000 pounds (6,804 kilograms)

Period: Cretaceous

Top Speed: 20 miles (32 kilometers) per hour

Number of Horns: 3

Best Defense: Massive head frill and huge horns

KOSMOCERATOPS

(koz-moh-SAYR-uh-tops)

Length: 15 feet (4.6 m)

Weight: 4,000 pounds (1,814 kg)

Period: Cretaceous

Top Speed: Unknown

Number of Horns: 15

Best Defense: Because it was smaller, it was probably faster than *Triceratops*.

CHAPTER 3

Keep Searching

Scientists are learning new things about dinosaurs every single day. In 2021, 42 new kinds of dinosaurs were named. One was a relative of *Triceratops*. It is called *Sierraceratops turneri* (see–ayr–uh–SAYR–uh–tops tur–NAYR–ee).

Sierraceratops was about 15 feet (4.6 m) long. Its skull alone measured 5 feet (1.5 m)! The dinosaur had horns above its eyes that were short but very wide. *Sierraceratops* lived about six million years before *Triceratops*.

Scientists discover new facts about ancient fossils using modern tools.

In 2015, scientists made an interesting discovery about *Triceratops* teeth. They used a machine called a micro tribometer. With it, they learned that *Triceratops* teeth had five different layers. Most reptile teeth have only two. This finding meant that *Triceratops* chompers must've been incredibly strong!

One exciting discovery from 2022 has people wondering if a great mystery may be solved soon. A well-preserved piece of *Triceratops* skin was found in North Dakota. The skin's color today is probably not the same as it was 66 million years ago. But scientists think they might be able to study the chemicals that make up the skin sample and then form a **hypothesis** about what the dinosaur's real color was.

Some *Triceratops* may have had up to 800 teeth.

Triceratops prorsus skull in left (top) and right (bottom

GLOSSARY

fossil (FAH–sul): the remains or traces of plants and animals that lived long ago

hypothesis (hy–POTH–eh–sihs): a guess you make based on information you already know

K–T extinction event (K T ek–STINGKT–shun ee–VENT): the time about 66 million years ago when nearly three–fourths of Earth's plant and animal life disappeared; some believe a giant space rock crashed into Earth and caused the event

paleontologist (pay–lee–on–TOL–uh–jist): a scientist who studies plants and animals that lived millions of years ago

prehistoric (pree–hiss–TORE–ick): belonging to a period in a time before written history

species (SPEE–sheez): a group of living things that are able to reproduce

theory (THEER–ee): a group of linked ideas intended to explain something

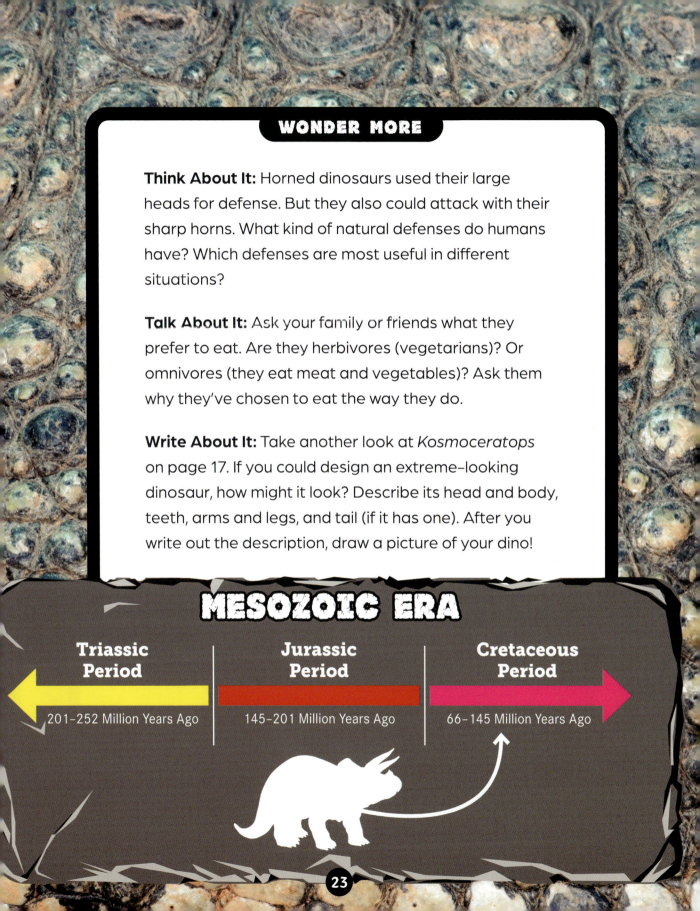

WONDER MORE

Think About It: Horned dinosaurs used their large heads for defense. But they also could attack with their sharp horns. What kind of natural defenses do humans have? Which defenses are most useful in different situations?

Talk About It: Ask your family or friends what they prefer to eat. Are they herbivores (vegetarians)? Or omnivores (they eat meat and vegetables)? Ask them why they've chosen to eat the way they do.

Write About It: Take another look at *Kosmoceratops* on page 17. If you could design an extreme–looking dinosaur, how might it look? Describe its head and body, teeth, arms and legs, and tail (if it has one). After you write out the description, draw a picture of your dino!

MESOZOIC ERA

Triassic Period
201–252 Million Years Ago

Jurassic Period
145–201 Million Years Ago

Cretaceous Period
66–145 Million Years Ago

LEARN MORE

BOOKS

Carr, Aaron. *Triceratops*. New York: AV2, 2022.

Kelly, Erin Suzanne. *Dinosaurs*. New York: Children's Press, 2021.

Sabelko, Rebecca. *Triceratops*. Minneapolis: Bellwether Media, 2020.

WEBSITES

Visit our website for links about *Triceratops*: **childsworld.com/links**

Note to Parents, Caregivers, Teachers, and Librarians: We routinely verify our web links to make sure they are safe and active sites. So encourage your readers to check them out!

INDEX